40 Sauces and Dressings Recipes for Home

By: Kelly Johnson

Table of Contents

- Classic Marinara Sauce
- Alfredo Sauce
- Pesto Sauce
- Bolognese Sauce
- Bechamel Sauce
- Hollandaise Sauce
- Chimichurri Sauce
- Teriyaki Sauce
- Hoisin Sauce
- Sweet and Sour Sauce
- Tahini Sauce
- Thai Peanut Sauce
- Mango Salsa
- Cilantro Lime Dressing
- Honey Mustard Sauce
- Caesar Dressing
- Blue Cheese Dressing
- Raspberry Vinaigrette
- Lemon Garlic Aioli
- Sriracha Mayo
- Caramelized Onion Gravy
- Chipotle Ranch Dressing
- Avocado Lime Crema
- Red Pepper Coulis
- Cranberry Orange Relish
- Cucumber Yogurt Sauce
- Sesame Ginger Glaze
- Red Wine Reduction
- Bourbon BBQ Sauce
- Miso Sesame Dressing
- Creamy Dill Sauce
- Roasted Garlic Mayo
- Basil Pesto Aioli
- Maple Dijon Vinaigrette
- Jalapeño Lime Marinade
- Sun-Dried Tomato Pesto

- Tzatziki Sauce
- Romesco Sauce
- Harissa Yogurt Sauce
- Pineapple Teriyaki Glaze

Classic Marinara Sauce

Ingredients:

- 2 tablespoons olive oil
- 1 onion, finely chopped
- 3 cloves garlic, minced
- 1 can (28 ounces) crushed tomatoes
- 1 can (14 ounces) diced tomatoes
- 1 teaspoon dried oregano
- 1 teaspoon dried basil
- 1/2 teaspoon dried thyme
- 1/2 teaspoon red pepper flakes (optional)
- Salt and black pepper to taste
- 1 teaspoon sugar (optional, to balance acidity)

Instructions:

Sauté Aromatics:

Heat olive oil in a saucepan over medium heat. Add finely chopped onions and sauté until translucent, about 5 minutes. Add minced garlic and cook for an additional 1-2 minutes, or until fragrant.

Add Tomatoes:

Pour in the crushed tomatoes and diced tomatoes with their juices. Stir to combine.

Season:

Add dried oregano, dried basil, dried thyme, red pepper flakes (if using), salt, and black pepper. Stir well to incorporate the seasonings into the sauce.

Simmer:

Bring the sauce to a gentle simmer. Reduce the heat to low and let it simmer for at least 30 minutes, stirring occasionally to prevent sticking. The longer it simmers, the richer the flavors will become.

Adjust Consistency and Seasoning:

> If the sauce is too thick, you can add a little water to achieve your desired consistency. Taste the sauce and adjust the seasoning, adding more salt, pepper or a touch of sugar to balance the acidity of the tomatoes.

Finish:

> Let the sauce cool slightly before serving. It can be used immediately or stored in an airtight container in the refrigerator for later use.

Serve:

> Use the Classic Marinara Sauce as a base for pasta dishes, pizzas, or as a dipping sauce for bread. Garnish with fresh basil or grated Parmesan cheese if desired.

This Classic Marinara Sauce is a versatile and timeless recipe that serves as a foundation for various Italian-inspired dishes. Its rich and savory flavor profile, combined with aromatic herbs, will elevate your meals to a new level of deliciousness.

Alfredo Sauce

Ingredients:

- 1/2 cup unsalted butter
- 2 cups heavy cream
- 2 cups Parmesan cheese, freshly grated
- 3 cloves garlic, minced
- Salt and black pepper to taste
- 1 pinch ground nutmeg (optional)
- Fresh parsley, chopped, for garnish

Instructions:

Melt Butter:

In a saucepan over medium heat, melt the unsalted butter.

Sauté Garlic:

Add minced garlic to the melted butter and sauté for about 1-2 minutes, or until fragrant. Be careful not to brown the garlic.

Pour in Cream:

Pour in the heavy cream, stirring continuously to combine it with the melted butter and garlic.

Simmer:

Allow the mixture to simmer gently for 2-3 minutes, letting it heat through without boiling.

Add Parmesan:

Gradually add the freshly grated Parmesan cheese to the sauce, stirring constantly. Continue stirring until the cheese is fully melted and the sauce becomes smooth and creamy.

Season:

Season the Alfredo sauce with salt and black pepper to taste. Add a pinch of ground nutmeg if desired for an extra layer of flavor.

Adjust Consistency:

If the sauce is too thick, you can adjust the consistency by adding a little more cream.

Finish and Garnish:

Once the sauce has reached the desired consistency and seasoning, remove it from heat. Garnish with freshly chopped parsley.

Serve:

Serve the Alfredo Sauce over your favorite pasta, such as fettuccine or linguine. It also pairs well with grilled chicken, shrimp, or vegetables.

Enjoy:

Indulge in the creamy goodness of homemade Alfredo Sauce, savoring the rich flavors and luxurious texture it adds to your dishes.

This homemade Alfredo Sauce s a classic and decadent addition to pasta dishes, providing a velvety texture and a delightful blend of garlic and Parmesan. Enjoy the comfort of restaurant-quality Alfredo in the convenience of your own kitchen!

Pesto Sauce

Ingredients:

- 2 cups fresh basil leaves, packed
- 1/2 cup freshly grated Parmesan cheese
- 1/2 cup pine nuts
- 3 cloves garlic, peeled
- 1 cup extra-virgin olive oil
- Salt and black pepper to taste
- 1/2 cup freshly grated Pecorino Romano cheese (optional)

Instructions:

Prepare Basil:

Wash and dry the fresh basil leaves, ensuring they are well-packed for a flavorful pesto.

Toast Pine Nuts:

In a dry skillet over medium heat, toast the pine nuts until lightly golden. Stir frequently and watch carefully to prevent burning. Remove from heat and let them cool.

Combine Ingredients:

In a food processor, combine the fresh basil, toasted pine nuts, freshly grated Parmesan cheese, and peeled garlic cloves.

Pulse:

Pulse the ingredients until coarsely chopped.

Drizzle Olive Oil:

With the food processor running, slowly drizzle in the extra-virgin olive oil until the mixture becomes a smooth paste.

Season:

Season the pesto with salt and black pepper to taste. Adjust the seasoning as needed.

Optional Pecorino Romano:

For an extra layer of flavor, you can add freshly grated Pecorino Romano cheese and pulse until combined.

Adjust Consistency:

If the pesto is too thick, you can add more olive oil to achieve your desired consistency.

Taste and Adjust:

Taste the pesto and adjust the salt, pepper, or cheese according to your preference.

Serve or Store:

Use the Pesto Sauce immediately as a pasta sauce, pizza topping, or sandwich spread. Alternatively, store it in an airtight container in the refrigerator for later use.

Enjoy:

Enjoy the vibrant and aromatic flavors of homemade Pesto Sauce, elevating your dishes with the freshness of basil, the richness of Parmesan, and the nuttiness of pine nuts.

Homemade Pesto Sauce is a versatile and vibrant addition to various dishes, adding a burst of fresh and herbaceous flavor. Use it to enhance pasta, sandwiches, or even as a flavorful drizzle over grilled vegetables.

Bolognese Sauce

Ingredients:

- 1 tablespoon olive oil
- 1 onion, finely chopped
- 2 carrots, finely diced
- 2 celery stalks, finely diced
- 3 cloves garlic, minced
- 1 pound (500g) ground beef
- 1/2 pound (250g) ground pork
- 1/2 cup red wine (optional)
- 2 cans (14 ounces each) crushed tomatoes
- 1/2 cup whole milk
- 1 teaspoon dried oregano
- 1 teaspoon dried basil
- 1/2 teaspoon dried thyme
- Salt and black pepper to taste
- Pinch of nutmeg (optional)
- 1/2 cup fresh parsley, chopped (for garnish)
- Grated Parmesan cheese (for serving)

Instructions:

Sauté Aromatics:

In a large, heavy-bottomed pot, heat olive oil over medium heat. Add finely chopped onions, diced carrots, and diced celery. Sauté until the vegetables are softened, about 5-7 minutes.

Add Garlic and Meat:

Add minced garlic and stir for 1-2 minutes until fragrant. Add ground beef and ground pork, breaking them apart with a spoon. Cook until the meat is browned and cooked through.

Deglaze with Wine (Optional):

Pour in the red wine (if using) and scrape any browned bits from the bottom of the pot. Allow the wine to simmer for a few minutes until it reduces slightly.

Add Tomatoes and Milk:

Add the crushed tomatoes and whole milk to the pot. Stir to combine.

Season and Simmer:

Add dried oregano, dried basil, dried thyme, salt, black pepper, and a pinch of nutmeg (if using). Stir well and bring the mixture to a simmer.

Simmer and Reduce:

Reduce the heat to low and let the Bolognese sauce simmer gently for at least 2 hours, stirring occasionally. The longer it simmers, the richer the flavors will become.

Adjust Seasoning:

Taste the sauce and adjust the seasoning if needed. Add more salt, pepper, or herbs according to your preference.

Finish and Garnish:

Just before serving, stir in chopped fresh parsley for a burst of freshness.

Serve:

Serve the Bolognese Sauce over your favorite pasta, such as tagliatelle or pappardelle. Garnish with grated Parmesan cheese.

Enjoy:

Indulge in the hearty and flavorful Bolognese Sauce, a classic Italian dish that promises a comforting and satisfying dining experience.

This Bolognese Sauce is a labor of love that results in a rich, meaty sauce with layers of savory flavors. Perfect for coating your favorite pasta, this traditional recipe will have you savoring the essence of Italian cuisine in every bite.

Bechamel Sauce

Ingredients:

- 4 tablespoons unsalted butter
- 1/4 cup all-purpose flour
- 2 cups whole milk, warmed
- Salt and white pepper to taste
- Pinch of ground nutmeg (optional)

Instructions:

Melt Butter:

In a saucepan over medium heat, melt the unsalted butter.

Add Flour:

Add the all-purpose flour to the melted butter, stirring continuously to create a smooth paste (roux). Cook the roux for 1-2 minutes, but avoid letting it brown.

Gradually Add Milk:

Gradually pour in the warmed whole milk while whisking continuously to avoid lumps. Keep whisking until the mixture is smooth and well combined.

Simmer:

Reduce the heat to low and let the sauce simmer gently. Continue stirring to prevent the sauce from sticking to the bottom of the pan.

Season:

Season the Béchamel sauce with salt and white pepper to taste. Add a pinch of ground nutmeg for a subtle, aromatic flavor (optional).

Cook to Desired Thickness:

Allow the sauce to cook and thicken to your desired consistency. This usually takes about 5-10 minutes. If the sauce becomes too thick, you can add a little more warmed milk.

Remove from Heat:

Once the Béchamel sauce has reached the desired thickness, remove it from the heat.

Strain (Optional):

For an extra smooth texture, you can strain the sauce through a fine-mesh sieve to remove any remaining lumps.

Use Immediately or Store:

Use the Béchamel sauce immediately in your recipe, or let it cool and store it in an airtight container in the refrigerator for later use.

Enjoy:

Enjoy the velvety and versatile Béchamel Sauce as a base for creamy pasta dishes, lasagna, gratins, or as a component in various culinary creations.

This Béchamel Sauce is a classic French sauce, known for its smooth and creamy consistency. Mastering this fundamental sauce opens the door to a variety of delicious dishes, making it an essential recipe in any kitchen.

Hollandaise Sauce

Ingredients:

- 3 large egg yolks
- 1 tablespoon water
- 1 tablespoon lemon juice
- 1 cup unsalted butter, melted
- Salt and cayenne pepper to taste

Instructions:

Prepare Double Boiler:

Fill the bottom of a double boiler with water, ensuring that it doesn't touch the top pan. Bring the water to a gentle simmer.

Whisk Egg Yolks:

In the top pan of the double boiler, whisk together the egg yolks, water, and lemon juice until well combined.

Cook Egg Mixture:

Place the top pan over the simmering water and continue to whisk the egg mixture continuously. Ensure that the water is simmering but not boiling.

Gradually Add Melted Butter:

Slowly drizzle in the melted butter while whisking vigorously. Keep whisking until the sauce thickens and doubles in volume. This should take about 5-8 minutes.

Season:

Season the Hollandaise sauce with salt and a pinch of cayenne pepper to taste. Adjust the seasoning as needed.

Remove from Heat:

Once the sauce has reached the desired thickness, remove the pan from the heat.

Serve Immediately:

Hollandaise sauce is best served immediately. Spoon it over eggs Benedict, asparagus, or your favorite dish.

Enjoy:

Indulge in the rich and velvety texture of homemade Hollandaise Sauce, adding a touch of luxury to your breakfast or brunch.

Note:

- If the sauce becomes too thick, you can thin it out by whisking in a little warm water.
- Be cautious not to overheat the sauce, as it can curdle. Keep the temperature low and steady throughout the process.

Mastering the art of Hollandaise sauce opens the door to elegant brunches and gourmet meals. Enjoy the creamy, buttery goodness of this classic sauce, perfect for elevating a variety of dishes.

Chimichurri Sauce

Ingredients:

- 1 cup fresh flat-leaf parsley, finely chopped
- 1/4 cup fresh cilantro, finely chopped
- 3 cloves garlic, minced
- 1/2 red onion, finely chopped
- 1 teaspoon dried oregano
- 1 teaspoon red pepper flakes (adjust to taste)
- 1/4 cup red wine vinegar
- 1/2 cup extra-virgin olive oil
- Salt and black pepper to taste

Instructions:

Prepare Herbs:

Finely chop the fresh flat-leaf parsley and cilantro.

Combine Ingredients:

In a bowl, combine the chopped parsley, chopped cilantro, minced garlic, finely chopped red onion, dried oregano, and red pepper flakes.

Add Vinegar:

Pour in the red wine vinegar and mix the ingredients together.

Drizzle Olive Oil:

Gradually drizzle in the extra-virgin olive oil while stirring the mixture.

Season:

Season the Chimichurri sauce with salt and black pepper to taste. Adjust the seasoning according to your preference.

Rest:

Allow the sauce to rest for at least 15-30 minutes before serving to let the flavors meld.

Adjust Consistency:

If the Chimichurri sauce is too thick, you can adjust the consistency by adding more olive oil.

Serve:

Serve the Chimichurri Sauce as a vibrant and flavorful condiment for grilled meats, poultry, seafood, or vegetables.

Enjoy:

Enjoy the zesty and herbaceous goodness of Chimichurri Sauce, bringing a burst of freshness to your favorite dishes.

Chimichurri Sauce is a versatile and bright condiment that hails from Argentina, known for its vibrant flavors and ability to enhance the taste of grilled or roasted dishes. Drizzle it over steaks, chicken, or grilled vegetables to add a delightful herbaceous kick to your meals.

Teriyaki Sauce

Ingredients:

- 1 cup soy sauce
- 1/2 cup water
- 1/4 cup rice vinegar
- 1/4 cup mirin (sweet rice wine)
- 1/4 cup brown sugar
- 3 tablespoons honey
- 3 cloves garlic, minced
- 1 tablespoon fresh ginger, grated
- 2 tablespoons cornstarch (optional, for thickening)
- 2 tablespoons water (optional, for cornstarch mixture)

Instructions:

Combine Ingredients:

In a saucepan, combine soy sauce, water, rice vinegar, mirin, brown sugar, honey, minced garlic, and grated ginger.

Simmer:

Bring the mixture to a simmer over medium heat. Stir occasionally to dissolve the sugar and let the flavors meld.

Taste and Adjust:

Taste the sauce and adjust the sweetness or saltiness according to your preference. Add more honey or soy sauce if needed.

Optional Thickening:

If you prefer a thicker sauce, mix cornstarch with water to create a slurry. Slowly pour the slurry into the simmering sauce while stirring continuously until the desired thickness is achieved.

Simmer and Infuse Flavors:

Let the sauce simmer for an additional 5-7 minutes, allowing it to thicken and the flavors to meld.

Cool:

Remove the sauce from heat and let it cool slightly. It will continue to thicken as it cools.

Store or Serve:

Once cooled, you can store the Teriyaki Sauce in a sealed container in the refrigerator for later use, or use it immediately.

Enjoy:

Use the homemade Teriyaki Sauce to glaze grilled chicken, beef, salmon, or vegetables, adding a savory-sweet flavor to your favorite dishes.

Homemade Teriyaki Sauce allows you to control the ingredients and tailor the flavor to your liking. Whether you use it as a marinade, glaze, or dipping sauce, this versatile condiment adds an irresistible umami kick to a variety of dishes.

Hoisin Sauce

Ingredients:

- 1/4 cup soy sauce
- 2 tablespoons peanut butter
- 1 tablespoon honey
- 1 tablespoon rice vinegar
- 1 tablespoon sesame oil
- 2 teaspoons garlic, minced
- 1 teaspoon ginger, grated
- 1 teaspoon Sriracha sauce (optional, for heat)
- 1 teaspoon cornstarch (optional, for thickening)
- 1 tablespoon water (optional, for cornstarch mixture)

Instructions:

Combine Ingredients:

In a bowl, whisk together soy sauce, peanut butter, honey, rice vinegar, sesame oil, minced garlic, grated ginger, and Sriracha sauce (if using).

Optional Thickening:

If you prefer a thicker consistency, mix cornstarch with water to create a slurry. Slowly whisk the slurry into the sauce until well combined.

Taste and Adjust:

Taste the Hoisin Sauce and adjust the sweetness or saltiness if necessary. You can add more honey or soy sauce based on your preference.

Store or Serve:

Transfer the Hoisin Sauce to a sealed container and refrigerate. The flavors will continue to meld over time.

Enjoy:

Use the homemade Hoisin Sauce as a dipping sauce, glaze for stir-fries, or marinade for meats. Enjoy the rich and savory-sweet flavors it adds to your dishes.

Homemade Hoisin Sauce allows you to create a personalized and flavorful condiment without artificial additives. Whether drizzling it over noodles, using it as a dipping sauce, or incorporating it into stir-fries, this versatile sauce brings depth and richness to a variety of Asian-inspired dishes.

Sweet and Sour Sauce

Ingredients:

- 1 cup pineapple juice
- 1/2 cup rice vinegar
- 1/4 cup ketchup
- 1/4 cup brown sugar
- 2 tablespoons soy sauce
- 1 tablespoon cornstarch
- 1 tablespoon water
- 1/2 cup pineapple chunks (optional)
- 1 bell pepper, diced
- 1 cup fresh or canned pineapple chunks (optional)

Instructions:

Combine Ingredients:

In a saucepan, whisk together pineapple juice, rice vinegar, ketchup, brown sugar, and soy sauce.

Bring to a Simmer:

Place the saucepan over medium heat and bring the mixture to a simmer, stirring frequently.

Optional Pineapple Chunks:

If using, add pineapple chunks and diced bell pepper to the sauce. Allow them to simmer along with the sauce until the bell pepper is tender.

Mix Cornstarch Slurry:

In a small bowl, mix cornstarch with water to create a slurry.

Thicken the Sauce:

Slowly pour the cornstarch slurry into the simmering sauce while stirring continuously. Continue to simmer until the sauce thickens to your desired consistency.

Adjust Sweetness:

Taste the Sweet and Sour Sauce and adjust the sweetness or acidity if needed. You can add more brown sugar for sweetness or more rice vinegar for acidity.

Optional Fresh Pineapple:

If using fresh pineapple chunks, add them to the sauce at the end. They will add a burst of freshness and natural sweetness.

Simmer and Finish:

Let the sauce simmer for an additional 2-3 minutes to allow the flavors to meld. Remove from heat.

Serve:

Serve the Sweet and Sour Sauce over your favorite protein, such as chicken, pork, or tofu. It also pairs well with rice or noodles.

Enjoy:

Enjoy the homemade Sweet and Sour Sauce, relishing the perfect balance of sweetness and tanginess it brings to your dishes.

Homemade Sweet and Sour Sauce is a versatile condiment that elevates a variety of dishes with its vibrant and balanced flavors. From stir-fries to dipping sauces, this recipe allows you to customize the sweetness and acidity according to your taste preferences.

Tahini Sauce

Ingredients:

- 1/2 cup tahini (sesame seed paste)
- 3 tablespoons lemon juice
- 2 tablespoons water
- 2 tablespoons olive oil
- 1 clove garlic, minced
- 1/2 teaspoon ground cumin
- Salt, to taste
- Fresh parsley, chopped (for garnish, optional)

Instructions:

Prepare Tahini:

Stir the tahini well before measuring to ensure it's thoroughly mixed.

Combine Ingredients:

In a bowl, whisk together tahini, lemon juice, water, olive oil, minced garlic, and ground cumin.

Adjust Consistency:

If the sauce is too thick, you can add more water, one tablespoon at a time, until you reach your desired consistency.

Season:

Season the Tahini Sauce with salt to taste. Keep in mind that the sauce will become more flavorful as it sits.

Mix Well:

Whisk the ingredients until the Tahini Sauce is smooth and well combined.

Rest:

Let the sauce rest for about 15 minutes to allow the flavors to meld. This also helps it to thicken slightly.

Garnish (Optional):

Garnish with chopped fresh parsley for a burst of freshness and color.

Serve:

Use the Tahini Sauce as a versatile condiment for various dishes. It complements falafel, grilled meats, vegetables, or can be used as a dressing for salads.

Store:

Store any leftover Tahini Sauce in an airtight container in the refrigerator. Stir well before using again.

Enjoy:

Enjoy the nutty and creamy flavor of homemade Tahini Sauce, enhancing the taste of your favorite dishes with its rich and versatile profile.

Tahini Sauce adds a delightful nuttiness and creaminess to a variety of dishes, making it a staple in Middle Eastern and Mediterranean cuisine. Drizzle it over your favorite dishes or use it as a dip to elevate your culinary creations.

Thai Peanut Sauce

Ingredients:

- 1/2 cup creamy peanut butter
- 3 tablespoons soy sauce
- 2 tablespoons rice vinegar
- 1 tablespoon sesame oil
- 1 tablespoon honey or maple syrup
- 1 clove garlic, minced
- 1 teaspoon fresh ginger, grated
- 1 teaspoon Sriracha sauce (adjust to taste)
- 3-4 tablespoons water (to thin, as needed)

Instructions:

Combine Ingredients:

In a bowl, whisk together creamy peanut butter, soy sauce, rice vinegar, sesame oil, honey or maple syrup, minced garlic, grated ginger, and Sriracha sauce.

Adjust Consistency:

Depending on your preference, add water gradually, one tablespoon at a time, to achieve the desired consistency. Whisk well after each addition.

Taste and Adjust:

Taste the Thai Peanut Sauce and adjust the flavors to your liking. You can add more soy sauce for saltiness, honey for sweetness, or Sriracha for heat.

Mix Well:

Whisk the ingredients until the sauce is smooth and well combined.

Rest:

Allow the sauce to rest for a few minutes to let the flavors meld. This will enhance the overall taste.

Adjust Consistency (Optional):

If the sauce thickens upon standing, you can add a bit more water and whisk to maintain the desired consistency.

Serve:

Use the Thai Peanut Sauce as a dipping sauce, drizzle it over noodles, or use it as a dressing for salads. It's also a fantastic accompaniment to satay or spring rolls.

Store:

Store any remaining sauce in an airtight container in the refrigerator. Stir well before using again.

Enjoy:

Enjoy the delightful blend of sweet, salty, and nutty flavors in this homemade Thai Peanut Sauce, bringing a taste of Thailand to your dishes.

This Thai Peanut Sauce is a versatile and flavorful condiment that adds a burst of taste to various dishes. Its rich and nutty profile complements a range of cuisines, making it a go-to sauce for those seeking a balance of sweet, salty, and spicy notes.

Mango Salsa

Ingredients:

- 2 ripe mangos, peeled, pitted, and diced
- 1 red bell pepper, diced
- 1/2 red onion, finely chopped
- 1 jalapeño, seeded and minced
- 1/4 cup fresh cilantro, chopped
- Juice of 2 limes
- Salt and pepper, to taste

Instructions:

Prepare Ingredients:

Peel, pit, and dice the ripe mangos. Dice the red bell pepper, finely chop the red onion, seed and mince the jalapeño, and chop the fresh cilantro.

Combine Ingredients:

In a bowl, combine the diced mango, diced red bell pepper, finely chopped red onion, minced jalapeño, and chopped cilantro.

Add Lime Juice:

Squeeze the juice of 2 limes over the mixture. Adjust the amount of lime juice based on your taste preference.

Season:

Season the Mango Salsa with salt and pepper to taste. Stir gently to combine all the ingredients.

Chill (Optional):

For enhanced flavors, you can refrigerate the salsa for about 30 minutes to allow the ingredients to meld.

Taste and Adjust:

Taste the salsa and adjust the seasoning or lime juice if needed.

Serve:

Serve the Mango Salsa as a refreshing side dish, topping for grilled meats or fish, or as a delicious dip with tortilla chips.

Enjoy:

Enjoy the vibrant and tropical flavors of homemade Mango Salsa, bringing a burst of freshness to your meals.

Mango Salsa is a colorful and delightful condiment that adds a tropical twist to your dishes. Whether served alongside grilled chicken, fish, or as a topping for tacos, its sweet and tangy flavors make it a versatile and refreshing addition to your culinary repertoire.

Cilantro Lime Dressing

Ingredients:

- 1 cup fresh cilantro leaves, packed
- 1/2 cup plain Greek yogurt
- 1/4 cup olive oil
- 2 cloves garlic, minced
- 2 tablespoons lime juice (adjust to taste)
- 1 teaspoon honey or maple syrup
- Salt and pepper, to taste

Instructions:

Prepare Ingredients:

Rinse and roughly chop the fresh cilantro leaves. Mince the garlic cloves.

Blend Cilantro:

In a blender or food processor, combine the chopped cilantro, plain Greek yogurt, olive oil, minced garlic, lime juice, and honey or maple syrup.

Blend Until Smooth:

Blend the ingredients until you achieve a smooth and creamy consistency.

Season:

Season the Cilantro Lime Dressing with salt and pepper to taste. Blend again to ensure the seasonings are well incorporated.

Taste and Adjust:

Taste the dressing and adjust the lime juice, honey or maple syrup, salt, or pepper to achieve the desired balance of flavors.

Chill (Optional):

For a colder and more refreshing dressing, you can refrigerate it for about 30 minutes before serving.

Serve:

Drizzle the Cilantro Lime Dressing over salads, grilled chicken, fish, or use it as a dip for vegetables.

Store:

Store any leftover dressing in a sealed container in the refrigerator for up to a week.

Enjoy:

Enjoy the zesty and herbaceous goodness of homemade Cilantro Lime Dressing, adding a burst of flavor to your favorite dishes.

This Cilantro Lime Dressing is a versatile and flavorful addition to salads, wraps, or as a marinade for grilled proteins. The combination of cilantro and lime creates a vibrant and refreshing dressing that elevates the taste of a variety of dishes.

Honey Mustard Sauce

Ingredients:

- 1/2 cup Dijon mustard
- 1/4 cup honey
- 2 tablespoons mayonnaise
- 1 tablespoon white vinegar
- Salt and pepper, to taste

Instructions:

Combine Ingredients:

In a bowl, whisk together Dijon mustard, honey, mayonnaise, and white vinegar.

Mix Thoroughly:

Whisk the ingredients until the mixture is smooth and well combined.

Season:

Season the Honey Mustard Sauce with salt and pepper to taste. Stir well to incorporate the seasonings.

Taste and Adjust:

Taste the sauce and adjust the sweetness or acidity by adding more honey or vinegar if desired.

Chill (Optional):

For a colder and thicker consistency, you can refrigerate the sauce for about 30 minutes before serving.

Serve:

Use the Honey Mustard Sauce as a dipping sauce for chicken tenders, pretzels, or vegetables. It also works well as a dressing for salads or as a glaze for grilled meats.

Store:

> Store any remaining sauce in an airtight container in the refrigerator for up to a week.

Enjoy:

> Enjoy the perfect balance of sweet and tangy flavors in this homemade Honey Mustard Sauce, enhancing a variety of dishes with its versatility.

Honey Mustard Sauce is a classic condiment that adds a delightful blend of sweetness and tanginess to your favorite snacks and meals. Whether used as a dip, dressing, or glaze, this homemade version allows you to tailor the flavors to suit your taste preferences.

Caesar Dressing

Ingredients:

- 1/2 cup mayonnaise
- 1/4 cup grated Parmesan cheese
- 2 tablespoons lemon juice
- 1 tablespoon Dijon mustard
- 1 clove garlic, minced
- 1 teaspoon Worcestershire sauce
- Salt and black pepper, to taste
- 1/4 cup extra-virgin olive oil

Instructions:

Combine Ingredients:

In a bowl, whisk together mayonnaise, grated Parmesan cheese, lemon juice, Dijon mustard, minced garlic, and Worcestershire sauce.

Season:

Season the Caesar Dressing with salt and black pepper to taste. Keep in mind that Parmesan cheese adds saltiness, so adjust accordingly.

Whisk in Olive Oil:

Slowly whisk in the extra-virgin olive oil until the dressing is well combined and has a smooth consistency.

Taste and Adjust:

Taste the dressing and adjust the lemon juice, salt, or pepper if needed. You can also add more olive oil for a thinner consistency.

Chill (Optional):

For optimal flavors, you can refrigerate the dressing for at least 30 minutes before serving.

Serve:

> Drizzle the Caesar Dressing over crisp romaine lettuce for a classic Caesar salad. It also works well as a dressing for chicken Caesar wraps or as a dip for crudités.

Store:

> Store any remaining dressing in an airtight container in the refrigerator for up to a week.

Enjoy:

> Enjoy the rich and savory flavors of homemade Caesar Dressing, elevating your salads and dishes with its creamy and zesty profile.

This Caesar Dressing recipe offers a creamy and flavorful dressing for your salads or wraps. The combination of Parmesan cheese, garlic, and lemon juice creates a classic Caesar flavor that pairs perfectly with crisp greens and various toppings.

Blue Cheese Dressing

Ingredients:

- 1/2 cup mayonnaise
- 1/4 cup sour cream
- 1/4 cup buttermilk
- 3 ounces blue cheese, crumbled
- 1 tablespoon white wine vinegar
- 1 clove garlic, minced
- 1/2 teaspoon Worcestershire sauce
- Salt and black pepper, to taste
- Fresh chives, chopped (for garnish, optional)

Instructions:

Combine Ingredients:

In a bowl, whisk together mayonnaise, sour cream, and buttermilk until well combined.

Add Blue Cheese:

Gently fold in the crumbled blue cheese, leaving some chunks for texture.

Mix in Flavorings:

Stir in white wine vinegar, minced garlic, and Worcestershire sauce.

Season:

Season the Blue Cheese Dressing with salt and black pepper to taste. Keep in mind that blue cheese is already salty, so adjust accordingly.

Chill (Optional):

For enhanced flavors, you can refrigerate the dressing for at least 30 minutes before serving.

Garnish (Optional):

Garnish the dressing with chopped fresh chives for added freshness and color.

Serve:

Use the Blue Cheese Dressing as a dip for chicken wings, a topping for salads, or a flavorful sauce for burgers.

Store:

Store any remaining dressing in an airtight container in the refrigerator for up to a week.

Enjoy:

Savor the bold and tangy taste of homemade Blue Cheese Dressing, bringing a rich and creamy element to your favorite dishes.

This Blue Cheese Dressing recipe offers a creamy and indulgent dressing that pairs perfectly with salads, wings, or as a delicious dip. The combination of tangy blue cheese, sour cream, and mayonnaise creates a flavorful dressing that adds a burst of richness to your meals.

Raspberry Vinaigrette

Ingredients:

- 1/2 cup fresh or frozen raspberries
- 3 tablespoons red wine vinegar
- 2 tablespoons honey or maple syrup
- 1/4 cup extra-virgin olive oil
- 1 teaspoon Dijon mustard
- Salt and black pepper, to taste

Instructions:

Prepare Raspberries:

If using frozen raspberries, let them thaw. If using fresh raspberries, rinse and drain them.

Blend Raspberries:

In a blender or food processor, blend the raspberries until smooth.

Strain (Optional):

For a smoother texture, you can strain the raspberry puree using a fine-mesh sieve to remove the seeds.

Combine Ingredients:

In a bowl, whisk together the raspberry puree, red wine vinegar, honey or maple syrup, and Dijon mustard.

Gradually Whisk in Olive Oil:

Gradually whisk in the extra-virgin olive oil until the vinaigrette is well emulsified.

Season:

Season the Raspberry Vinaigrette with salt and black pepper to taste. Adjust the sweetness or acidity as needed.

Chill (Optional):

    For enhanced flavors, you can refrigerate the vinaigrette for about 30 minutes before serving.

Serve:

    Drizzle the Raspberry Vinaigrette over salads with mixed greens, goat cheese, and nuts. It also works well with grilled chicken or as a marinade.

Store:

    Store any remaining vinaigrette in an airtight container in the refrigerator for up to a week.

Enjoy:

    Enjoy the vibrant and fruity flavors of homemade Raspberry Vinaigrette, adding a burst of freshness to your salads and dishes.

This Raspberry Vinaigrette recipe offers a delightful balance of sweet and tangy flavors, making it a perfect dressing for salads. The natural sweetness of raspberries combined with the acidity of red wine vinegar creates a refreshing vinaigrette that enhances the taste of your favorite greens.

Lemon Garlic Aioli

Ingredients:

- 1 cup mayonnaise
- 2 cloves garlic, minced
- 2 tablespoons fresh lemon juice
- 1 teaspoon lemon zest
- 1/2 teaspoon Dijon mustard
- Salt and black pepper, to taste
- 2 tablespoons fresh parsley, finely chopped (optional, for garnish)

Instructions:

Mince Garlic:

    Finely mince the garlic cloves.

Zest and Juice Lemon:

    Zest the lemon to get about 1 teaspoon of lemon zest. Squeeze the lemon to obtain 2 tablespoons of fresh lemon juice.

Combine Ingredients:

    In a bowl, whisk together mayonnaise, minced garlic, lemon juice, lemon zest, and Dijon mustard.

Season:

    Season the Lemon Garlic Aioli with salt and black pepper to taste. Adjust the seasoning according to your preference.

Mix Well:

    Whisk the ingredients until the aioli is smooth and well combined.

Chill (Optional):

For optimal flavors, you can refrigerate the aioli for about 30 minutes before serving.

Garnish (Optional):

If desired, garnish the Lemon Garlic Aioli with finely chopped fresh parsley for added freshness and color.

Serve:

Use the Lemon Garlic Aioli as a dipping sauce for fries, a spread for sandwiches, or a flavorful accompaniment for seafood.

Store:

Store any remaining aioli in an airtight container in the refrigerator for up to a week.

Enjoy:

Enjoy the zesty and garlicky goodness of homemade Lemon Garlic Aioli, enhancing a variety of dishes with its creamy and tangy profile.

This Lemon Garlic Aioli recipe brings together the bold flavors of garlic and the bright zestiness of lemon, creating a versatile and delicious condiment. Whether used as a dip, spread, or sauce, this aioli adds a burst of citrusy and garlicky goodness to your favorite meals.

Sriracha Mayo

Ingredients:

- 1/2 cup mayonnaise
- 1 tablespoon Sriracha sauce (adjust to taste)
- 1 teaspoon soy sauce
- 1 teaspoon rice vinegar
- 1 teaspoon honey or maple syrup (optional, for sweetness)
- 1/2 teaspoon garlic powder
- 1/2 teaspoon onion powder (optional)
- Sesame seeds and chopped green onions (for garnish, optional)

Instructions:

Combine Ingredients:

In a bowl, whisk together mayonnaise, Sriracha sauce, soy sauce, rice vinegar, honey or maple syrup (if using), garlic powder, and onion powder (if using).

Adjust Heat:

Taste the Sriracha Mayo and adjust the Sriracha sauce quantity based on your preferred level of spiciness.

Mix Well:

Whisk the ingredients until the Sriracha Mayo is smooth and well combined.

Adjust Sweetness (Optional):

If you prefer a slightly sweet flavor, add more honey or maple syrup and whisk again.

Chill (Optional):

For enhanced flavors, you can refrigerate the Sriracha Mayo for about 30 minutes before serving.

Garnish (Optional):

> If desired, garnish the Sriracha Mayo with sesame seeds and chopped green onions for added texture and freshness.

Serve:

> Use the Sriracha Mayo as a dipping sauce for fries, a spread for sandwiches, or a zesty topping for grilled meats and seafood.

Store:

> Store any remaining Sriracha Mayo in an airtight container in the refrigerator for up to a week.

Enjoy:

> Enjoy the spicy and creamy kick of homemade Sriracha Mayo, adding a bold flavor to your favorite dishes.

This Sriracha Mayo recipe provides a perfect balance of creaminess and spiciness, making it a versatile condiment for various dishes. Whether used as a dip, spread, or sauce, this homemade version allows you to tailor the heat level and flavors to suit your taste preferences.

Caramelized Onion Gravy

Ingredients:

- 2 large onions, thinly sliced
- 3 tablespoons butter
- 2 tablespoons all-purpose flour
- 2 cups beef or vegetable broth
- 1/2 cup red wine (optional)
- 1 teaspoon Worcestershire sauce
- Salt and black pepper, to taste
- Fresh thyme or rosemary (optional, for garnish)

Instructions:

Caramelize Onions:

In a large skillet, melt 2 tablespoons of butter over medium heat. Add the thinly sliced onions and cook, stirring occasionally, until the onions are deeply golden brown and caramelized. This process may take about 20-30 minutes.

Make Roux:

Push the caramelized onions to one side of the skillet, add the remaining tablespoon of butter to the empty side, and let it melt. Sprinkle the flour over the melted butter and stir to create a roux. Cook the roux for 1-2 minutes to remove the raw flour taste.

Combine Onions and Roux:

Gradually incorporate the caramelized onions into the roux, stirring to combine.

Deglaze with Wine (Optional):

If using red wine, pour it into the skillet to deglaze, scraping up any browned bits from the bottom. Allow the wine to reduce for a few minutes.

Add Broth:

Slowly pour in the broth while stirring continuously to avoid lumps. Continue stirring until the mixture thickens.

Season:

Add Worcestershire sauce and season the gravy with salt and black pepper to taste. Adjust the seasoning as needed.

Simmer:

Let the gravy simmer over low heat for 5-10 minutes to allow the flavors to meld and the consistency to thicken.

Garnish (Optional):

If desired, garnish the Caramelized Onion Gravy with fresh thyme or rosemary for additional aroma and flavor.

Serve:

Serve the Caramelized Onion Gravy over mashed potatoes, roasted meats, or your favorite comfort food.

Enjoy:

Enjoy the rich and savory goodness of homemade Caramelized Onion Gravy, adding a layer of flavor to your dishes.

This Caramelized Onion Gravy recipe transforms humble onions into a rich and flavorful topping for various dishes. Whether paired with mashed potatoes, roasted meats, or even sandwiches, the deep caramelization adds a sweet and savory depth to this classic gravy.

Chipotle Ranch Dressing

Ingredients:

- 1 cup mayonnaise
- 1/2 cup buttermilk
- 1-2 chipotle peppers in adobo sauce (adjust to taste)
- 1 tablespoon adobo sauce (from the chipotle pepper can)
- 2 tablespoons fresh cilantro, chopped
- 1 tablespoon fresh lime juice
- 1 teaspoon garlic powder
- 1 teaspoon onion powder
- 1/2 teaspoon dried dill
- Salt and black pepper, to taste

Instructions:

Prepare Chipotle Peppers:

Finely chop 1-2 chipotle peppers from the can, adjusting the quantity based on your preferred level of spiciness.

Blend Ingredients:

In a blender or food processor, combine mayonnaise, buttermilk, chopped chipotle peppers, adobo sauce, fresh cilantro, fresh lime juice, garlic powder, onion powder, dried dill, salt, and black pepper.

Blend Until Smooth:

Blend the ingredients until the Chipotle Ranch Dressing is smooth and well combined.

Adjust Consistency:

If the dressing is too thick, you can add more buttermilk, a tablespoon at a time, until you reach the desired consistency.

Taste and Adjust:

Taste the dressing and adjust the chipotle peppers, lime juice, or seasoning according to your preference.

Chill (Optional):

For optimal flavors, you can refrigerate the dressing for about 30 minutes before serving.

Serve:

Use the Chipotle Ranch Dressing as a zesty dip for vegetables, a flavorful dressing for salads, or a tasty sauce for tacos and wraps.

Store:

Store any remaining dressing in an airtight container in the refrigerator for up to a week.

Enjoy:

Enjoy the smoky, spicy, and creamy goodness of homemade Chipotle Ranch Dressing, adding a bold kick to your favorite dishes.

This Chipotle Ranch Dressing recipe combines the smoky heat of chipotle peppers with the cool creaminess of ranch dressing, creating a versatile and flavorful condiment. Whether used as a dip, dressing, or sauce, this homemade version allows you to customize the spice level to suit your taste preferences.

Avocado Lime Crema

Ingredients:

- 1 ripe avocado, peeled and pitted
- 1/2 cup sour cream
- 2 tablespoons fresh lime juice
- 1 clove garlic, minced
- 1 tablespoon fresh cilantro, chopped
- Salt and black pepper, to taste

Instructions:

Prepare Avocado:

Peel and pit the ripe avocado.

Mash Avocado:

In a bowl, mash the avocado using a fork or spoon until smooth.

Combine Ingredients:

Add sour cream, fresh lime juice, minced garlic, and chopped cilantro to the mashed avocado.

Season:

Season the Avocado Lime Crema with salt and black pepper to taste. Adjust the seasoning according to your preference.

Mix Well:

Mix the ingredients thoroughly until the crema is smooth and well combined.

Adjust Consistency (Optional):

If you prefer a thinner consistency, you can add a little more lime juice or sour cream and mix again.

Chill (Optional):

> For enhanced flavors, you can refrigerate the crema for about 30 minutes before serving.

Serve:

> Use the Avocado Lime Crema as a topping for tacos, quesadillas, grilled meats, or as a dip for tortilla chips.

Store:

> Store any remaining crema in an airtight container in the refrigerator for up to a day. The lime juice helps preserve the color of the avocado.

Enjoy:

> Enjoy the creamy and zesty goodness of homemade Avocado Lime Crema, adding a burst of flavor to your favorite Mexican-inspired dishes.

This Avocado Lime Crema recipe combines the richness of avocado with the tangy freshness of lime, creating a versatile and delicious topping. Whether used as a condiment for tacos or a dip for snacks, this crema adds a delightful creaminess and flavor to your culinary creations.

Red Pepper Coulis

Ingredients:

- 2 large red bell peppers, roasted, peeled, and seeded
- 1 tablespoon olive oil
- 1 small onion, finely chopped
- 2 cloves garlic, minced
- 1 cup vegetable or chicken broth
- Salt and black pepper, to taste
- Fresh basil or parsley, chopped (for garnish, optional)

Instructions:

Roast Red Peppers:

Preheat your oven's broiler. Place the red bell peppers on a baking sheet and broil, turning occasionally, until the skin is charred and blistered. Transfer the peppers to a bowl, cover with plastic wrap, and let them steam for about 10 minutes. Peel off the skin, remove seeds, and chop the roasted peppers.

Sauté Onion and Garlic:

In a saucepan, heat olive oil over medium heat. Add chopped onion and sauté until softened, about 3-4 minutes. Add minced garlic and cook for an additional 1-2 minutes until fragrant.

Add Roasted Peppers:

Add the chopped roasted red peppers to the saucepan, stirring to combine with the onion and garlic.

Cook and Blend:

Pour in the vegetable or chicken broth and bring the mixture to a simmer. Cook for about 10 minutes to allow the flavors to meld. Use an immersion blender or transfer the mixture to a blender to puree until smooth.

Strain (Optional):

For a smoother consistency, you can strain the coulis using a fine-mesh sieve to remove any remaining pulp.

Season:

Season the Red Pepper Coulis with salt and black pepper to taste. Adjust the seasoning according to your preference.

Garnish (Optional):

If desired, garnish the coulis with chopped fresh basil or parsley for added freshness.

Serve:

Serve the Red Pepper Coulis as a vibrant sauce for grilled meats, fish, or vegetables. It can also be used as a flavorful base for soups or drizzled over pasta.

Store:

Store any remaining coulis in an airtight container in the refrigerator for up to a week.

Enjoy:

Enjoy the rich and velvety texture of homemade Red Pepper Coulis, adding a burst of color and flavor to your dishes.

This Red Pepper Coulis recipe offers a versatile and flavorful sauce that can elevate various dishes. Whether used as a vibrant topping for proteins or as a base for soups, the roasted red peppers bring a sweet and smoky depth to this delightful coulis.

Cranberry Orange Relish

Ingredients:

- 1 bag (12 ounces) fresh or frozen cranberries
- 1 medium orange, zest and juice
- 3/4 cup granulated sugar (adjust to taste)
- 1/4 cup water
- 1/4 teaspoon ground cinnamon
- 1/4 teaspoon ground ginger
- Pinch of salt
- Optional: 1/2 cup chopped nuts (walnuts or pecans)

Instructions:

Prepare Ingredients:

Rinse the cranberries under cold water and remove any stems or debris. Zest the orange and then juice it.

Cook Cranberries:

In a saucepan, combine cranberries, orange zest, orange juice, granulated sugar, water, ground cinnamon, ground ginger, and a pinch of salt.

Simmer:

Bring the mixture to a boil over medium-high heat, then reduce the heat to low. Simmer, stirring occasionally, until the cranberries burst and the mixture thickens, about 10-15 minutes.

Adjust Sweetness:

Taste the relish and adjust the sweetness by adding more sugar if needed. Keep in mind that the relish will continue to thicken as it cools.

Optional Nuts:

If using, stir in chopped nuts (walnuts or pecans) for added texture and flavor.

Cool:

> Allow the Cranberry Orange Relish to cool to room temperature. It will continue to thicken as it cools.

Chill (Optional):

> For optimal flavors, you can refrigerate the relish for at least 1-2 hours before serving.

Serve:

> Serve the Cranberry Orange Relish as a side dish for turkey, ham, or roast chicken. It can also be used as a topping for desserts like cheesecake or as a spread for sandwiches.

Store:

> Store any remaining relish in an airtight container in the refrigerator for up to a week.

Enjoy:

> Enjoy the sweet and tart goodness of homemade Cranberry Orange Relish, adding a burst of flavor to your holiday meals and beyond.

This Cranberry Orange Relish recipe combines the tartness of fresh cranberries with the citrusy sweetness of orange, creating a vibrant and flavorful condiment. Whether served alongside your holiday feast or used creatively in other dishes, this relish adds a delightful zing to your culinary repertoire.

Cucumber Yogurt Sauce

Ingredients:

- 1 cucumber, peeled, seeded, and finely diced
- 1 cup plain Greek yogurt
- 2 tablespoons fresh mint, finely chopped
- 1 clove garlic, minced
- 1 tablespoon extra-virgin olive oil
- 1 tablespoon lemon juice
- Salt and black pepper, to taste

Instructions:

Prepare Cucumber:

Peel the cucumber, cut it in half lengthwise, and use a spoon to scoop out the seeds. Finely dice the cucumber.

Combine Ingredients:

In a bowl, combine the diced cucumber, plain Greek yogurt, chopped fresh mint, minced garlic, extra-virgin olive oil, and lemon juice.

Season:

Season the Cucumber Yogurt Sauce with salt and black pepper to taste. Adjust the seasoning according to your preference.

Mix Well:

Mix the ingredients thoroughly until the sauce is well combined.

Chill (Optional):

For enhanced flavors, you can refrigerate the sauce for about 30 minutes before serving.

Serve:

Use the Cucumber Yogurt Sauce as a refreshing dip for vegetables, a topping for grilled meats, or a sauce for gyros and wraps.

Store:

Store any remaining sauce in an airtight container in the refrigerator for up to a day.

Enjoy:

Enjoy the cool and tangy goodness of homemade Cucumber Yogurt Sauce, adding a burst of freshness to your dishes.

This Cucumber Yogurt Sauce recipe offers a light and refreshing condiment that complements a variety of dishes. Whether used as a dip, dressing, or sauce, the combination of cucumber, yogurt, and mint creates a delightful balance of flavors that pairs well with both appetizers and main courses.

Sesame Ginger Glaze

Ingredients:

- 3 tablespoons soy sauce
- 2 tablespoons rice vinegar
- 1 tablespoon sesame oil
- 2 tablespoons honey
- 1 tablespoon fresh ginger, grated
- 1 clove garlic, minced
- 1 teaspoon cornstarch (optional, for thickening)
- 1 tablespoon water (optional, for thinning)
- Toasted sesame seeds (for garnish, optional)
- Sliced green onions (for garnish, optional)

Instructions:

Prepare Ginger:

Peel and grate the fresh ginger. Mince the garlic.

Combine Ingredients:

In a bowl, whisk together soy sauce, rice vinegar, sesame oil, honey, grated ginger, and minced garlic.

Thicken (Optional):

If you prefer a thicker glaze, mix cornstarch with water to create a slurry. Add it to the sauce and whisk well. Heat the mixture in a saucepan over low heat until it thickens. Allow it to cool.

Thin (Optional):

If you want a thinner consistency, you can add a tablespoon of water to the glaze and whisk until well combined.

Garnish (Optional):

If desired, garnish the Sesame Ginger Glaze with toasted sesame seeds and sliced green onions for added texture and flavor.

Chill (Optional):

For enhanced flavors, you can refrigerate the glaze for about 30 minutes before using.

Serve:

Use the Sesame Ginger Glaze as a marinade for grilled chicken, shrimp, or vegetables. It also works well as a drizzle for stir-fries or a dipping sauce for spring rolls.

Store:

Store any remaining glaze in an airtight container in the refrigerator for up to a week.

Enjoy:

Enjoy the savory-sweet goodness of homemade Sesame Ginger Glaze, elevating the flavor of your favorite dishes.

This Sesame Ginger Glaze recipe provides a versatile and flavorful sauce that adds a delicious Asian-inspired touch to your meals. Whether used as a marinade, drizzle, or dipping sauce, the combination of soy sauce, sesame, and ginger creates a savory-sweet profile that enhances the taste of various dishes.

Red Wine Reduction

Ingredients:

- 1 cup red wine (choose a good-quality red wine)
- 1/4 cup shallots, finely chopped
- 1 tablespoon olive oil
- 1 cup beef or vegetable broth
- 1 tablespoon unsalted butter
- 1 teaspoon fresh thyme leaves
- Salt and black pepper, to taste

Instructions:

Sauté Shallots:

In a saucepan, heat olive oil over medium heat. Add finely chopped shallots and sauté until they become translucent.

Add Red Wine:

Pour in the red wine, stirring to combine with the sautéed shallots. Bring the mixture to a simmer.

Reduce Wine:

Allow the red wine to simmer and reduce by about half. This process intensifies the flavor of the wine.

Add Broth:

Pour in the beef or vegetable broth, stirring to combine. Let the mixture simmer for an additional 10-15 minutes to further reduce and concentrate the flavors.

Strain (Optional):

For a smoother sauce, you can strain the reduction using a fine-mesh sieve to remove any solid pieces.

Finish with Butter:

Stir in unsalted butter until it melts into the sauce, adding richness and a smooth finish.

Season:

Season the Red Wine Reduction Sauce with fresh thyme leaves, salt, and black pepper to taste. Adjust the seasoning according to your preference.

Serve:

Drizzle the Red Wine Reduction Sauce over grilled meats, roasted vegetables, or your favorite dishes.

Store:

Store any remaining sauce in an airtight container in the refrigerator for up to a week. Reheat gently before serving.

Enjoy:

Enjoy the deep and savory flavors of homemade Red Wine Reduction Sauce, elevating the taste of your dishes with a touch of elegance.

This Red Wine Reduction Sauce recipe creates a rich and luxurious sauce that pairs well with various meats and dishes. The reduction process concentrates the flavors of the wine and broth, resulting in a versatile sauce that adds depth and sophistication to your culinary creations.

Bourbon BBQ Sauce

Ingredients:

- 1 cup ketchup
- 1/2 cup bourbon whiskey
- 1/4 cup apple cider vinegar
- 1/4 cup brown sugar, packed
- 2 tablespoons Worcestershire sauce
- 1 tablespoon Dijon mustard
- 1 teaspoon smoked paprika
- 1 teaspoon onion powder
- 1 teaspoon garlic powder
- 1/2 teaspoon black pepper
- 1/2 teaspoon salt

Instructions:

Combine Ingredients:

In a saucepan, combine ketchup, bourbon whiskey, apple cider vinegar, brown sugar, Worcestershire sauce, Dijon mustard, smoked paprika, onion powder, garlic powder, black pepper, and salt.

Mix Well:

Whisk the ingredients together until well combined.

Simmer:

Place the saucepan over medium heat and bring the mixture to a simmer. Reduce the heat to low to maintain a gentle simmer.

Cook and Thicken:

Allow the Bourbon BBQ Sauce to simmer for about 15-20 minutes, stirring occasionally. This helps the flavors meld and the sauce to thicken.

Adjust Consistency (Optional):

If you prefer a thicker sauce, continue simmering until it reaches your desired consistency. If it's too thick, you can add a splash of water to thin it out.

Taste and Adjust:

Taste the BBQ sauce and adjust the seasoning if needed. You can add more brown sugar for sweetness or adjust the salt and pepper to your liking.

Cool:

Allow the Bourbon BBQ Sauce to cool to room temperature.

Store:

Transfer the sauce to a jar or airtight container and store it in the refrigerator.

Serve:

Use the Bourbon BBQ Sauce as a glaze for grilled meats, a dipping sauce for chicken wings, or a flavorful condiment for burgers and sandwiches.

Enjoy:

Enjoy the sweet, smoky, and rich flavors of homemade Bourbon BBQ Sauce, adding a touch of bourbon-infused goodness to your favorite barbecue dishes.

This Bourbon BBQ Sauce recipe brings together the sweet and smoky notes of bourbon with classic barbecue flavors. It's a versatile sauce that can enhance the taste of grilled and smoked meats, providing a rich and flavorful addition to your barbecue repertoire.

Miso Sesame Dressing

Ingredients:

- 3 tablespoons white miso paste
- 2 tablespoons rice vinegar
- 1 tablespoon soy sauce
- 1 tablespoon sesame oil
- 1 tablespoon honey or maple syrup
- 1 teaspoon fresh ginger, grated
- 1 clove garlic, minced
- 2 tablespoons neutral oil (such as vegetable or grapeseed oil)
- 1 tablespoon sesame seeds, toasted (for garnish, optional)
- Water (to adjust consistency, if needed)

Instructions:

Combine Ingredients:

In a bowl, whisk together white miso paste, rice vinegar, soy sauce, sesame oil, honey or maple syrup, grated ginger, and minced garlic.

Emulsify with Oil:

While whisking continuously, slowly drizzle in the neutral oil to emulsify the dressing.

Adjust Consistency:

If the dressing is too thick, you can adjust the consistency by adding water, a tablespoon at a time, until you reach the desired thickness.

Taste and Adjust:

Taste the Miso Sesame Dressing and adjust the flavors as needed. You can add more honey or soy sauce based on your preference.

Garnish (Optional):

If desired, garnish the dressing with toasted sesame seeds for added texture and nuttiness.

Chill (Optional):

For enhanced flavors, you can refrigerate the dressing for about 30 minutes before serving.

Serve:

Use the Miso Sesame Dressing as a flavorful topping for salads, a dipping sauce for sushi, or a marinade for grilled vegetables and proteins.

Store:

Store any remaining dressing in an airtight container in the refrigerator for up to a week.

Enjoy:

Enjoy the umami-rich and nutty flavors of homemade Miso Sesame Dressing, adding a depth of taste to your favorite dishes.

This Miso Sesame Dressing recipe combines the savory umami of miso with the nutty richness of sesame, creating a versatile and flavorful dressing. Whether drizzled over salads, used as a marinade, or as a dipping sauce, this homemade dressing adds a unique and delicious twist to your culinary creations.

Creamy Dill Sauce

Ingredients:

- 1 cup mayonnaise
- 2 tablespoons sour cream
- 2 tablespoons fresh dill, finely chopped
- 1 tablespoon Dijon mustard
- 1 tablespoon white wine vinegar or lemon juice
- 1 clove garlic, minced
- Salt and black pepper, to taste
- Water (to adjust consistency, if needed)

Instructions:

Combine Ingredients:

In a bowl, mix together mayonnaise, sour cream, finely chopped fresh dill, Dijon mustard, white wine vinegar or lemon juice, and minced garlic.

Blend Well:

Whisk the ingredients until well combined, ensuring that the dill is evenly distributed throughout the sauce.

Adjust Consistency:

If the sauce is too thick for your liking, you can adjust the consistency by adding water, a tablespoon at a time, until you achieve the desired thickness.

Season:

Season the Creamy Dill Sauce with salt and black pepper to taste. Adjust the seasoning based on your preference.

Chill (Optional):

For optimal flavors, you can refrigerate the sauce for about 30 minutes before serving.

Serve:

> Use the Creamy Dill Sauce as a refreshing dip for seafood, a topping for grilled fish, or a sauce for sandwiches and wraps.

Store:

> Store any remaining sauce in an airtight container in the refrigerator for up to a week.

Enjoy:

> Enjoy the cool and herby goodness of homemade Creamy Dill Sauce, adding a burst of flavor to your dishes.

This Creamy Dill Sauce recipe provides a delightful balance of tanginess and freshness. Whether paired with seafood, grilled proteins, or used as a dressing, the combination of dill, mayonnaise, and sour cream creates a versatile and delicious condiment.

Roasted Garlic Mayo

Ingredients:

- 1 cup mayonnaise
- 1 head of garlic
- 1 tablespoon olive oil
- 1 tablespoon lemon juice
- Salt and black pepper, to taste

Instructions:

Roast Garlic:

Preheat the oven to 400°F (200°C). Cut off the top of the garlic head to expose the cloves. Place the garlic head on a piece of foil, drizzle with olive oil, and wrap it in the foil. Roast in the preheated oven for about 40-45 minutes, or until the garlic cloves are soft and golden brown.

Squeeze Roasted Garlic:

Allow the roasted garlic to cool slightly. Squeeze the roasted garlic cloves out of their skins into a bowl.

Make Roasted Garlic Mayo:

In a separate bowl, combine mayonnaise, the squeezed roasted garlic, lemon juice, salt, and black pepper.

Blend Well:

Use a fork or whisk to blend the ingredients thoroughly until the roasted garlic is evenly incorporated into the mayo.

Adjust Seasoning:

Taste the Roasted Garlic Mayo and adjust the seasoning, adding more salt, pepper, or lemon juice to suit your preference.

Chill (Optional):

For enhanced flavors, you can refrigerate the Roasted Garlic Mayo for about 30 minutes before serving.

Serve:

Use the Roasted Garlic Mayo as a flavorful spread for sandwiches, a dipping sauce for fries, or a creamy topping for grilled meats.

Store:

Store any remaining Roasted Garlic Mayo in an airtight container in the refrigerator for up to a week.

Enjoy:

Enjoy the rich and savory goodness of homemade Roasted Garlic Mayo, adding a depth of flavor to your favorite dishes.

This Roasted Garlic Mayo recipe transforms regular mayonnaise into a flavorful and aromatic spread. The roasted garlic brings a mellow sweetness and depth, making it a versatile condiment for a variety of dishes.

Basil Pesto Aioli

Ingredients:

- 1 cup mayonnaise
- 2 tablespoons basil pesto
- 1 clove garlic, minced
- 1 tablespoon lemon juice
- Salt and black pepper, to taste

Instructions:

Prepare Basil Pesto:

If you don't have store-bought basil pesto, you can make a simple one by blending fresh basil leaves, garlic, pine nuts, Parmesan cheese, and olive oil in a food processor.

Make Basil Pesto Aioli:

In a bowl, combine mayonnaise, basil pesto, minced garlic, and lemon juice.

Blend Well:

Use a fork or whisk to blend the ingredients thoroughly until the basil pesto is evenly incorporated into the aioli.

Season:

Season the Basil Pesto Aioli with salt and black pepper to taste. Adjust the seasoning based on your preference.

Chill (Optional):

For optimal flavors, you can refrigerate the aioli for about 30 minutes before serving.

Serve:

Use the Basil Pesto Aioli as a flavorful dip for vegetables, a spread for sandwiches, or a sauce for grilled meats and seafood.

Store:

Store any remaining Basil Pesto Aioli in an airtight container in the refrigerator for up to a week.

Enjoy:

Enjoy the vibrant and herby goodness of homemade Basil Pesto Aioli, adding a burst of flavor to your dishes.

This Basil Pesto Aioli recipe combines the rich and aromatic flavors of basil pesto with the creamy goodness of aioli. Whether used as a dip, spread, or sauce, this homemade condiment adds a delicious twist to a variety of dishes.

Maple Dijon Vinaigrette

Ingredients:

- 1/4 cup extra-virgin olive oil
- 2 tablespoons balsamic vinegar
- 1 tablespoon Dijon mustard
- 1 tablespoon maple syrup
- 1 clove garlic, minced (optional)
- Salt and black pepper, to taste

Instructions:

Combine Ingredients:

In a bowl, whisk together extra-virgin olive oil, balsamic vinegar, Dijon mustard, and maple syrup.

Add Garlic (Optional):

If desired, add minced garlic to the vinaigrette for an extra layer of flavor. Whisk to combine.

Season:

Season the Maple Dijon Vinaigrette with salt and black pepper to taste. Adjust the seasoning based on your preference.

Whisk Well:

Whisk the ingredients thoroughly until the vinaigrette is well combined and has a smooth consistency.

Chill (Optional):

For enhanced flavors, you can refrigerate the vinaigrette for about 30 minutes before serving.

Serve:

Use the Maple Dijon Vinaigrette as a dressing for salads, a marinade for grilled vegetables or proteins, or a flavorful sauce for roasted dishes.

Store:

Store any remaining vinaigrette in an airtight container in the refrigerator for up to a week.

Enjoy:

Enjoy the sweet and tangy goodness of homemade Maple Dijon Vinaigrette, elevating the taste of your favorite dishes.

This Maple Dijon Vinaigrette recipe combines the bold flavor of Dijon mustard with the sweetness of maple syrup, creating a versatile dressing that adds depth to salads and dishes. Whether used as a marinade or a sauce, this homemade vinaigrette brings a delightful balance of sweet and tangy notes to your culinary creations.

Jalapeño Lime Marinade

Ingredients:

- 1/4 cup olive oil
- Zest and juice of 2 limes
- 2 tablespoons chopped fresh cilantro
- 1 jalapeño, seeded and finely chopped
- 2 cloves garlic, minced
- 1 teaspoon honey or agave syrup
- 1 teaspoon ground cumin
- Salt and black pepper, to taste

Instructions:

Prepare Ingredients:

Zest and juice the limes. Finely chop the jalapeño, removing the seeds for less heat. Chop fresh cilantro and mince the garlic.

Combine Ingredients:

In a bowl, mix together olive oil, lime zest, lime juice, chopped cilantro, chopped jalapeño, minced garlic, honey or agave syrup, ground cumin, salt, and black pepper.

Whisk Well:

Whisk the ingredients thoroughly to ensure that the marinade is well combined.

Adjust Heat (Optional):

If you prefer a spicier marinade, you can leave some or all of the jalapeño seeds in. Taste the marinade and adjust the heat level accordingly.

Marinate:

Place your choice of protein (chicken, shrimp, tofu, etc.) in a resealable plastic bag or shallow dish. Pour the Jalapeño Lime Marinade over the protein, making sure it is well-coated. Marinate in the refrigerator for at least 30 minutes, or longer for more flavor.

Grill or Cook:

Remove the protein from the marinade and grill, bake, or cook as desired.

Serve:

Serve the grilled or cooked protein with additional fresh lime wedges and a sprinkle of cilantro for garnish.

Store:

Store any leftover marinade in an airtight container in the refrigerator for up to a week.

Enjoy:

Enjoy the zesty and spicy kick of homemade Jalapeño Lime Marinade, adding a burst of flavor to your grilled dishes.

This Jalapeño Lime Marinade recipe combines the citrusy tang of lime with the heat of jalapeño, creating a flavorful and zesty marinade for your favorite proteins. Whether used for grilling, baking, or cooking, this homemade marinade adds a delicious and spicy kick to your dishes.

Sun-Dried Tomato Pesto

Ingredients:

- 1 cup sun-dried tomatoes (dry-packed or oil-packed), drained
- 1/2 cup fresh basil leaves
- 1/2 cup grated Parmesan cheese
- 1/3 cup pine nuts or walnuts
- 2 cloves garlic, minced
- 1/2 cup extra-virgin olive oil
- 1 tablespoon lemon juice
- Salt and black pepper, to taste

Instructions:

Rehydrate Sun-Dried Tomatoes:

If you're using dry-packed sun-dried tomatoes, rehydrate them by soaking in hot water for about 15-20 minutes. If using oil-packed tomatoes, drain them.

Combine Ingredients:

In a food processor, combine the rehydrated sun-dried tomatoes, fresh basil leaves, grated Parmesan cheese, pine nuts or walnuts, and minced garlic.

Process Until Coarse:

Pulse the ingredients until they form a coarse mixture.

Add Olive Oil and Lemon Juice:

With the food processor running, gradually add the extra-virgin olive oil and lemon juice. Continue processing until the pesto reaches your desired consistency.

Season:

Season the Sun-Dried Tomato Pesto with salt and black pepper to taste. Adjust the seasoning based on your preference.

Scrape Down Sides (Optional):

If needed, stop the food processor and scrape down the sides to ensure all ingredients are well incorporated.

Taste and Adjust:

Taste the pesto and adjust the flavors, adding more lemon juice, salt, or pepper as needed.

Serve:

Use the Sun-Dried Tomato Pesto as a flavorful sauce for pasta, a spread for sandwiches, or a topping for grilled proteins.

Store:

Store any remaining pesto in an airtight container in the refrigerator. You can also drizzle a layer of olive oil on top to help preserve its freshness.

Enjoy:

Enjoy the rich and savory goodness of homemade Sun-Dried Tomato Pesto, adding a burst of flavor to your favorite dishes.

This Sun-Dried Tomato Pesto recipe combines the intense sweetness of sun-dried tomatoes with the aromatic freshness of basil, creating a versatile and flavorful condiment. Whether tossed with pasta, used as a spread, or incorporated into various dishes, this homemade pesto adds a delicious and vibrant twist to your culinary creations.

Tzatziki Sauce

Ingredients:

- 1 cucumber, seeded and finely grated
- 1 cup Greek yogurt
- 2 cloves garlic, minced
- 1 tablespoon extra-virgin olive oil
- 1 tablespoon fresh dill, chopped
- 1 tablespoon fresh mint, chopped (optional)
- 1 tablespoon lemon juice
- Salt and black pepper, to taste

Instructions:

Prepare Cucumber:

Peel and seed the cucumber. Finely grate the cucumber using a box grater or a food processor.

Drain Cucumber:

Place the grated cucumber in a fine-mesh sieve or cheesecloth over a bowl. Sprinkle with a pinch of salt and let it drain for about 15-20 minutes to remove excess moisture.

Combine Ingredients:

In a bowl, combine the drained grated cucumber, Greek yogurt, minced garlic, extra-virgin olive oil, chopped fresh dill, chopped fresh mint (if using), and lemon juice.

Mix Well:

Mix the ingredients thoroughly until well combined.

Season:

Season the Tzatziki Sauce with salt and black pepper to taste. Adjust the seasoning based on your preference.

Chill (Optional):

> For enhanced flavors, you can refrigerate the Tzatziki Sauce for about 30 minutes before serving.

Serve:

> Use the Tzatziki Sauce as a refreshing dip for pita bread, a sauce for grilled meats, or a topping for gyros and salads.

Store:

> Store any remaining Tzatziki Sauce in an airtight container in the refrigerator for up to a week.

Enjoy:

> Enjoy the cool and tangy goodness of homemade Tzatziki Sauce, adding a burst of flavor to your Mediterranean-inspired dishes.

This Tzatziki Sauce recipe offers a creamy and flavorful condiment that complements a variety of dishes. Whether served with grilled meats, used as a dip, or incorporated into wraps, the combination of cucumber, yogurt, and herbs creates a refreshing and versatile sauce.

Romesco Sauce

Ingredients:

- 1 cup roasted red bell peppers, drained (from a jar or freshly roasted)
- 1/2 cup almonds, toasted
- 2 cloves garlic, peeled
- 1/4 cup fresh flat-leaf parsley
- 2 tablespoons red wine vinegar
- 1 teaspoon smoked paprika
- 1/2 teaspoon cayenne pepper (adjust to taste)
- 1/2 cup extra-virgin olive oil
- Salt and black pepper, to taste

Instructions:

Roast Red Bell Peppers:

If using fresh bell peppers, roast them until the skin is charred. Allow them to cool, peel off the skin, and remove the seeds. If using jarred roasted red bell peppers, drain them.

Toast Almonds:

In a dry pan, toast the almonds over medium heat until they are lightly browned and fragrant. Stir frequently to avoid burning. Allow them to cool.

Combine Ingredients:

In a food processor, combine the roasted red bell peppers, toasted almonds, garlic, fresh parsley, red wine vinegar, smoked paprika, and cayenne pepper.

Process Until Smooth:

Pulse the ingredients until they form a coarse mixture. Then, with the food processor running, gradually pour in the extra-virgin olive oil until the mixture becomes a smooth sauce.

Season:

Season the Romesco Sauce with salt and black pepper to taste. Adjust the seasoning based on your preference.

Taste and Adjust:

Taste the sauce and adjust the flavors, adding more vinegar, paprika, or cayenne pepper if desired.

Chill (Optional):

For enhanced flavors, you can refrigerate the Romesco Sauce for about 30 minutes before serving.

Serve:

Use the Romesco Sauce as a flavorful dip for bread, a sauce for grilled vegetables, or a condiment for roasted meats.

Store:

Store any remaining Romesco Sauce in an airtight container in the refrigerator for up to a week.

Enjoy:

Enjoy the rich and nutty goodness of homemade Romesco Sauce, adding a burst of flavor to your dishes.

This Romesco Sauce recipe brings together the bold flavors of roasted red peppers, toasted almonds, and aromatic spices, creating a versatile and delicious sauce. Whether used as a dip, spread, or accompaniment to grilled dishes, this homemade Romesco Sauce adds a unique and savory twist to your culinary creations.

Harissa Yogurt Sauce

Ingredients:

- 1 cup Greek yogurt
- 2 tablespoons harissa paste
- 1 tablespoon extra-virgin olive oil
- 1 tablespoon lemon juice
- 1 clove garlic, minced
- 1 teaspoon ground cumin
- Salt and black pepper, to taste
- Fresh cilantro or mint, chopped (for garnish, optional)

Instructions:

Combine Ingredients:

In a bowl, whisk together Greek yogurt, harissa paste, extra-virgin olive oil, lemon juice, minced garlic, and ground cumin.

Whisk Until Smooth:

Whisk the ingredients until the harissa paste is evenly incorporated into the yogurt, and the mixture becomes smooth.

Season:

Season the Harissa Yogurt Sauce with salt and black pepper to taste. Adjust the seasoning based on your preference.

Adjust Heat (Optional):

Taste the sauce and, if you desire more heat, you can add additional harissa paste.

Chill (Optional):

For enhanced flavors, you can refrigerate the Harissa Yogurt Sauce for about 30 minutes before serving.

Serve:

> Use the Harissa Yogurt Sauce as a spicy dip for vegetables, a sauce for grilled meats, or a flavorful topping for tacos and sandwiches.

Garnish (Optional):

> If desired, garnish the sauce with chopped fresh cilantro or mint for added freshness.

Store:

> Store any remaining Harissa Yogurt Sauce in an airtight container in the refrigerator for up to a week.

Enjoy:

> Enjoy the creamy and spicy goodness of homemade Harissa Yogurt Sauce, adding a kick of flavor to your dishes.

This Harissa Yogurt Sauce recipe combines the creaminess of Greek yogurt with the bold and spicy flavors of harissa, creating a versatile and flavorful sauce. Whether used as a dip, spread, or condiment, this homemade sauce adds a delightful heat to a variety of dishes.

Pineapple Teriyaki Glaze

Ingredients:

- 1 cup pineapple juice
- 1/4 cup soy sauce
- 2 tablespoons brown sugar
- 2 tablespoons rice vinegar
- 1 tablespoon mirin (sweet rice wine) or dry sherry
- 1 teaspoon fresh ginger, grated
- 1 teaspoon garlic, minced
- 1 tablespoon cornstarch (optional, for thickening)
- 2 tablespoons water (optional, for thinning)

Instructions:

Combine Ingredients:

In a saucepan, combine pineapple juice, soy sauce, brown sugar, rice vinegar, mirin or dry sherry, grated ginger, and minced garlic.

Whisk and Simmer:

Whisk the ingredients together and bring the mixture to a simmer over medium heat.

Simmer and Reduce:

Allow the Pineapple Teriyaki Glaze to simmer and reduce for about 10-15 minutes, or until it reaches the desired thickness. Stir occasionally to prevent sticking.

Check Consistency:

If the glaze is too thick for your liking, you can mix cornstarch with water to create a slurry. Gradually add the slurry to the glaze while stirring continuously until it reaches the desired consistency.

Adjust Sweetness (Optional):

Taste the glaze and, if needed, adjust the sweetness by adding more brown sugar.

Cool and Thicken (Optional):

Allow the glaze to cool for a few minutes. It will continue to thicken as it cools. If it becomes too thick, you can thin it out by adding a bit of water.

Use:

Brush the Pineapple Teriyaki Glaze over grilled chicken, pork, seafood, or vegetables during the last few minutes of cooking. It can also be used as a dipping sauce.

Store:

Store any remaining glaze in an airtight container in the refrigerator for up to a week.

Enjoy:

Enjoy the sweet and tangy goodness of homemade Pineapple Teriyaki Glaze, adding a tropical twist to your grilled dishes.

This Pineapple Teriyaki Glaze recipe combines the sweetness of pineapple juice with the savory notes of teriyaki, creating a delicious glaze for grilled meats and vegetables. Whether used as a marinade or a finishing sauce, this homemade glaze adds a burst of flavor to your favorite dishes.

www.ingramcontent.com/pod-product-compliance
Lightning Source LLC
LaVergne TN
LVHW061946070526
838199LV00060B/3995